# Communion

## Guitar Solos Appropriate for Eucharistic Worship

## By William Bay

To *access* the online audio recording go to:
WWW.MELBAY.COM/WBM66MEB

# *Preface*

Communion is one of the most important and sacred elements of Christian worship. I have always thought that the addition of worshipful and prayerful music during the eucharistic celebration adds meaning for each participant. This is a collection of 24 guitar solos in notation and tablature which are worshipful in nature and lend themselves appropriately to the service of communion. All solos are recorded and can be accessed at the URL on the title page of this book. I hope you enjoy listening to them and find opportunity to play them in worship.

*William Bay*

# Contents

# My Faith Look Up to Thee
## Olivet

Lowell Mason

4

# Nearer, My God, to Thee
## *Bethany*

*Dropped-D Tuning*

Lowell Mason

D
21
26
31
7

# Let Us Break Bread Together

# Lord, Speak to Me
## *Canonbury*

Robert Schumann

# Just As I Am
## Woodworth

William Bradbury

B
21
26
26
31
31
36
36

# Jesu, Joy of Man's Desiring

J. S. Bach

# Have Thine Own Way, Lord
### *Adelaide*

George C. Stebbins

**Relaxed Tempo**

B
25
31
31
38
38
rit.
45
45

# My Shepherd Will Supply My Need
## *Resignation*

Southern Harmony, 1835

# Praxis Pietatis Melica

Johann Crueger, 1653

**Moderato**

D

# Jesus Spreads His Banner O'er Us

## *Autumn*

*Jesus spreads his banner o'er us, Cheers our famished souls with food;*
*In thy fasting and temptation, In thy labors on the earth,*
*Precious banquet, bread of heaven, Wine of gladness, flowing free,*
*May we taste it, kindly given, In remembrance, Lord, of thee.*

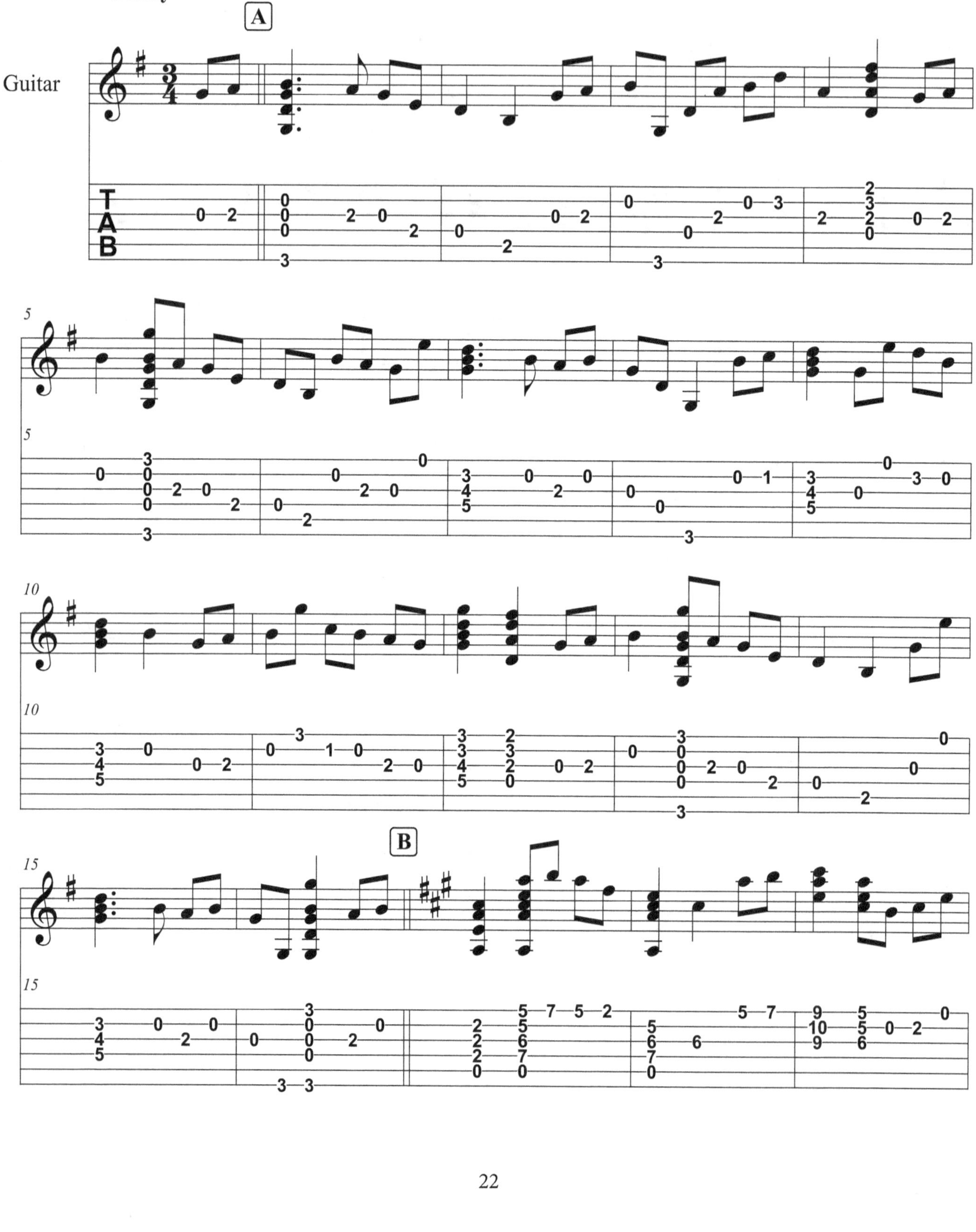

# Rendez Á Dieu

**Reverently**

Louis Bourgeois, 1543

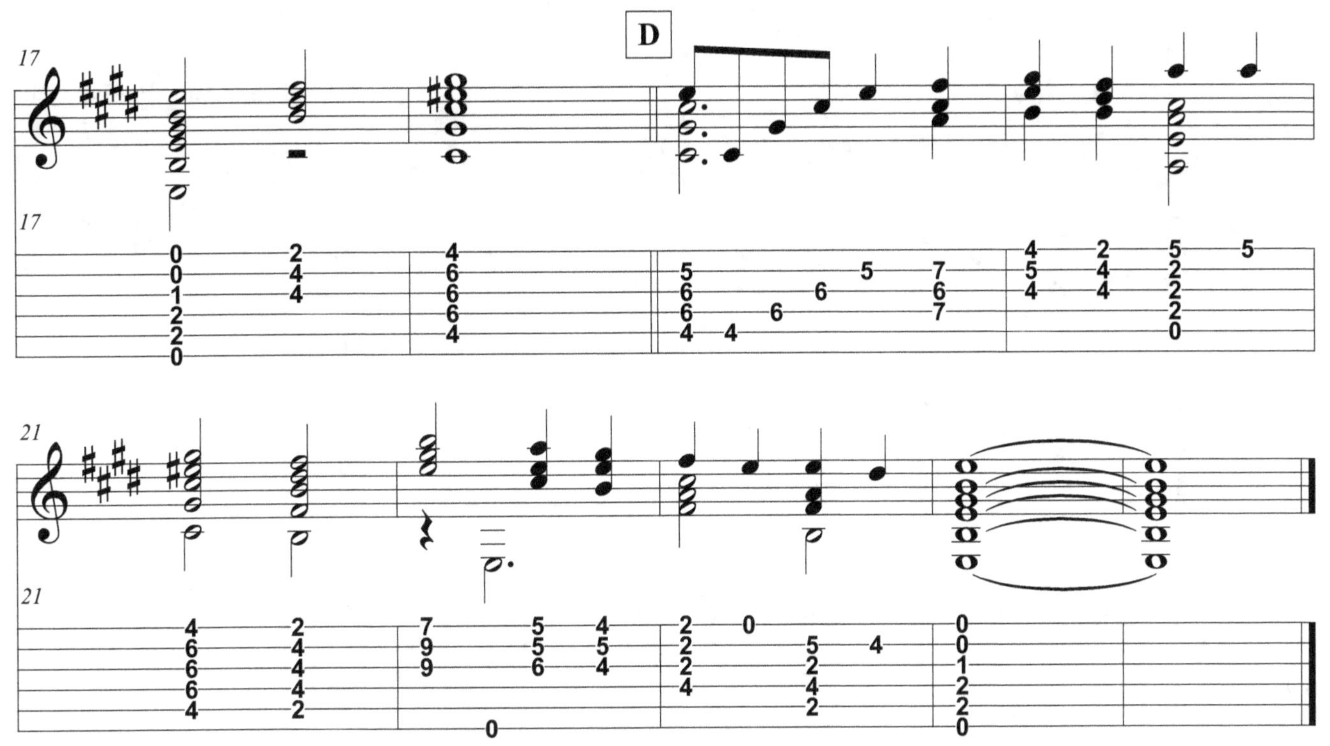

# O Esca Viatorum

**Gently**

Louis Bourgeois, 1549

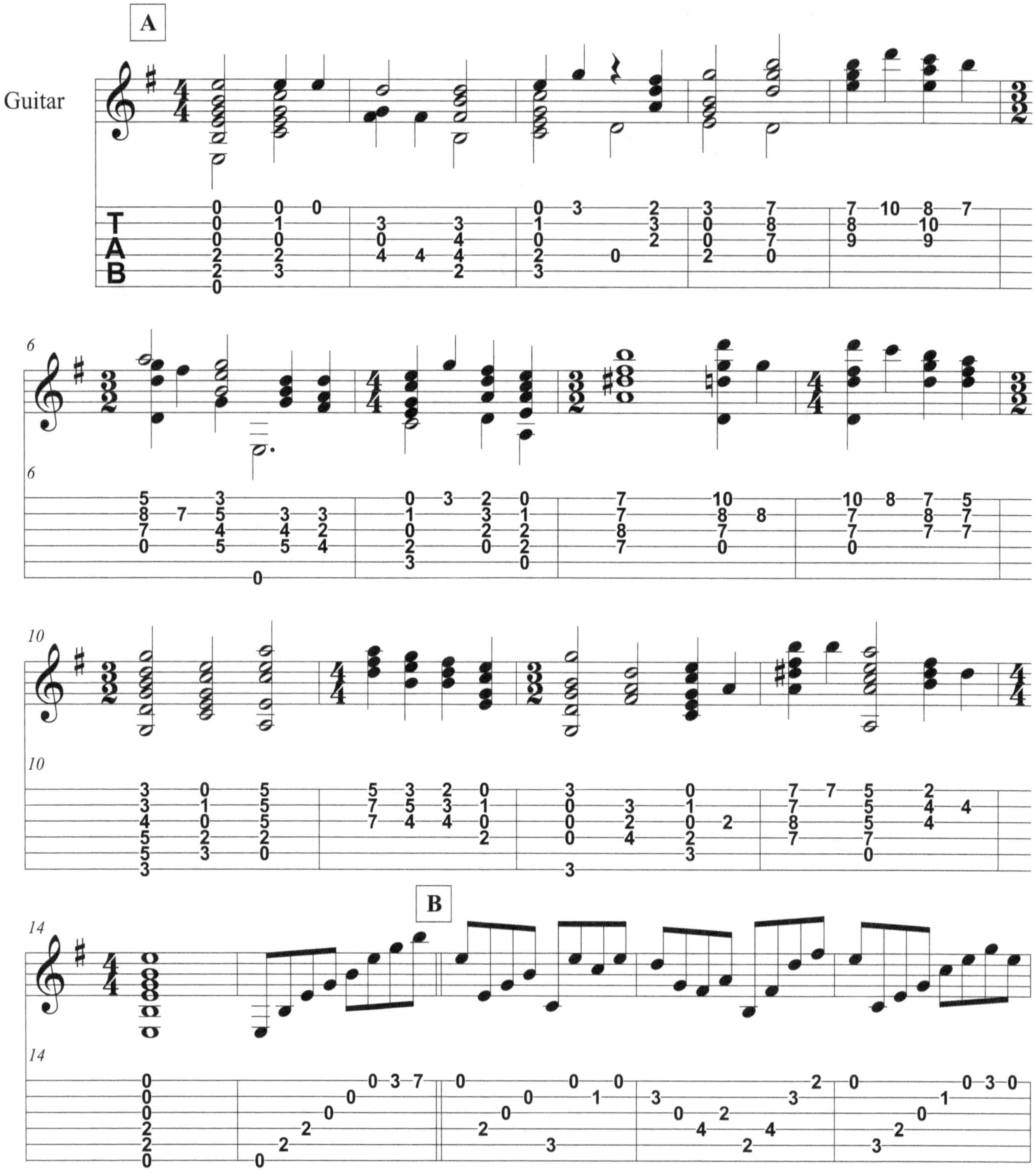

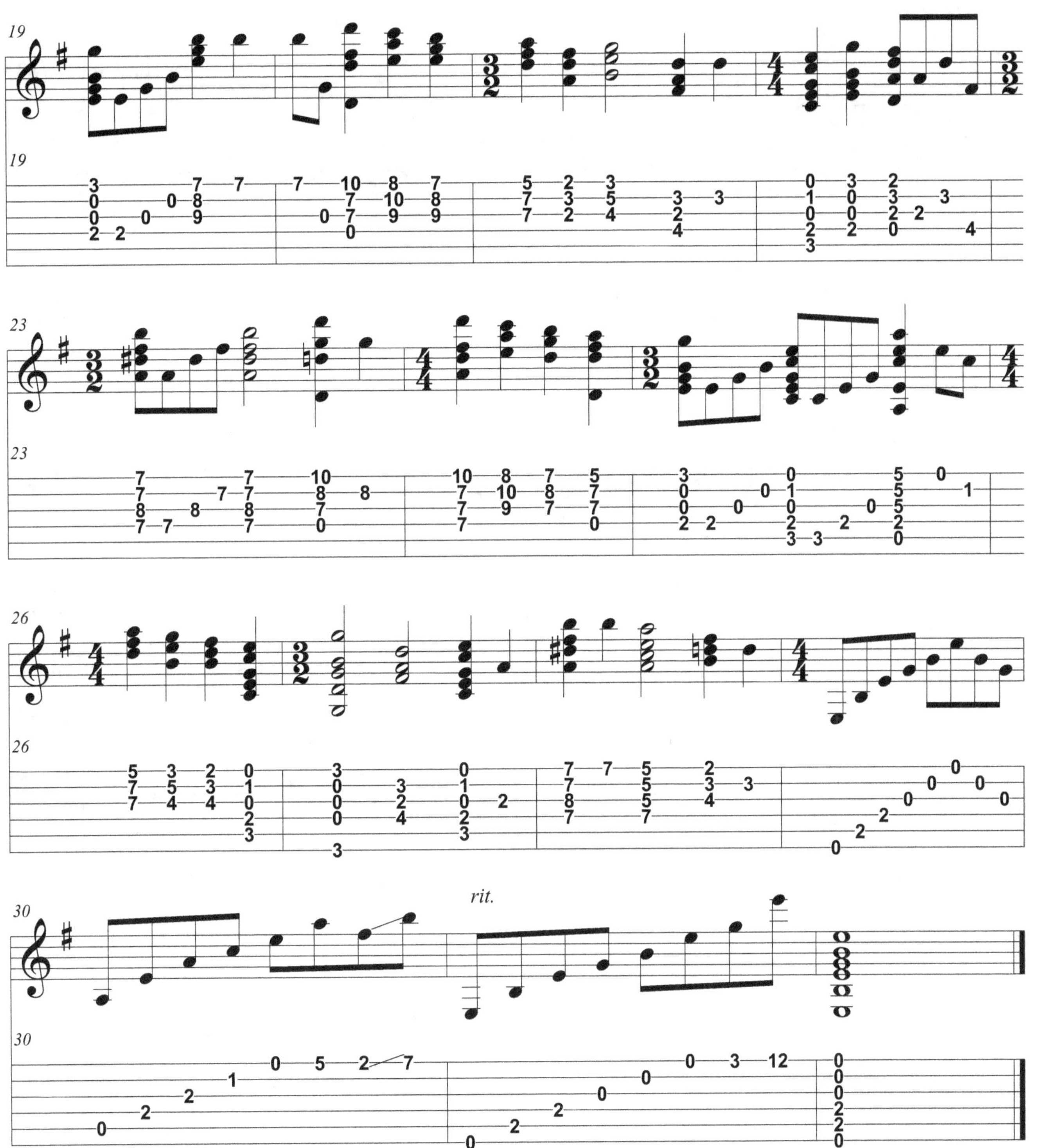

# I Will Arise and Go to Jesus
## *Arise*

# The Lord's Supper
## *Way*

**Gently**

William Bay

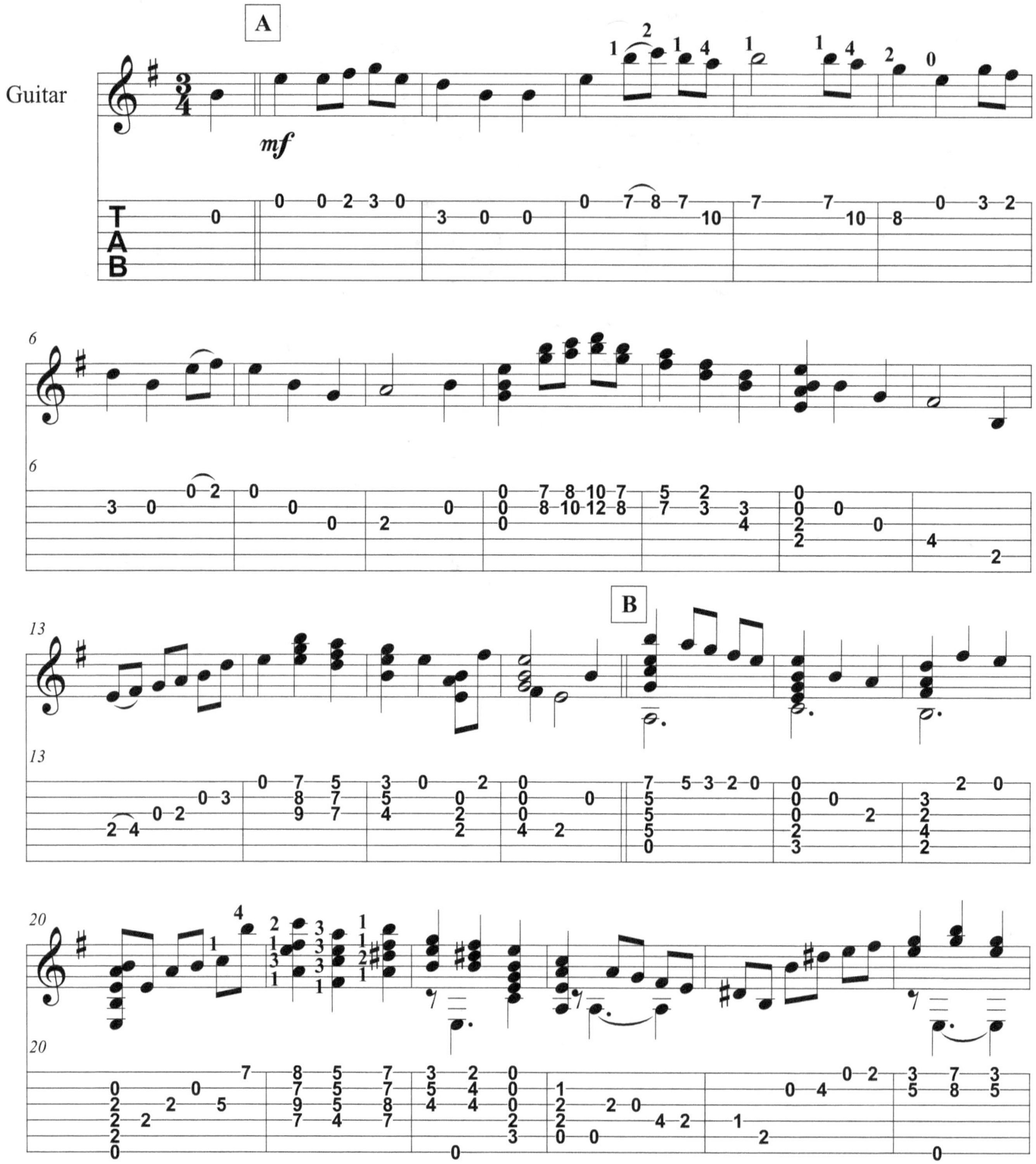

F
G

# Come to the Feast



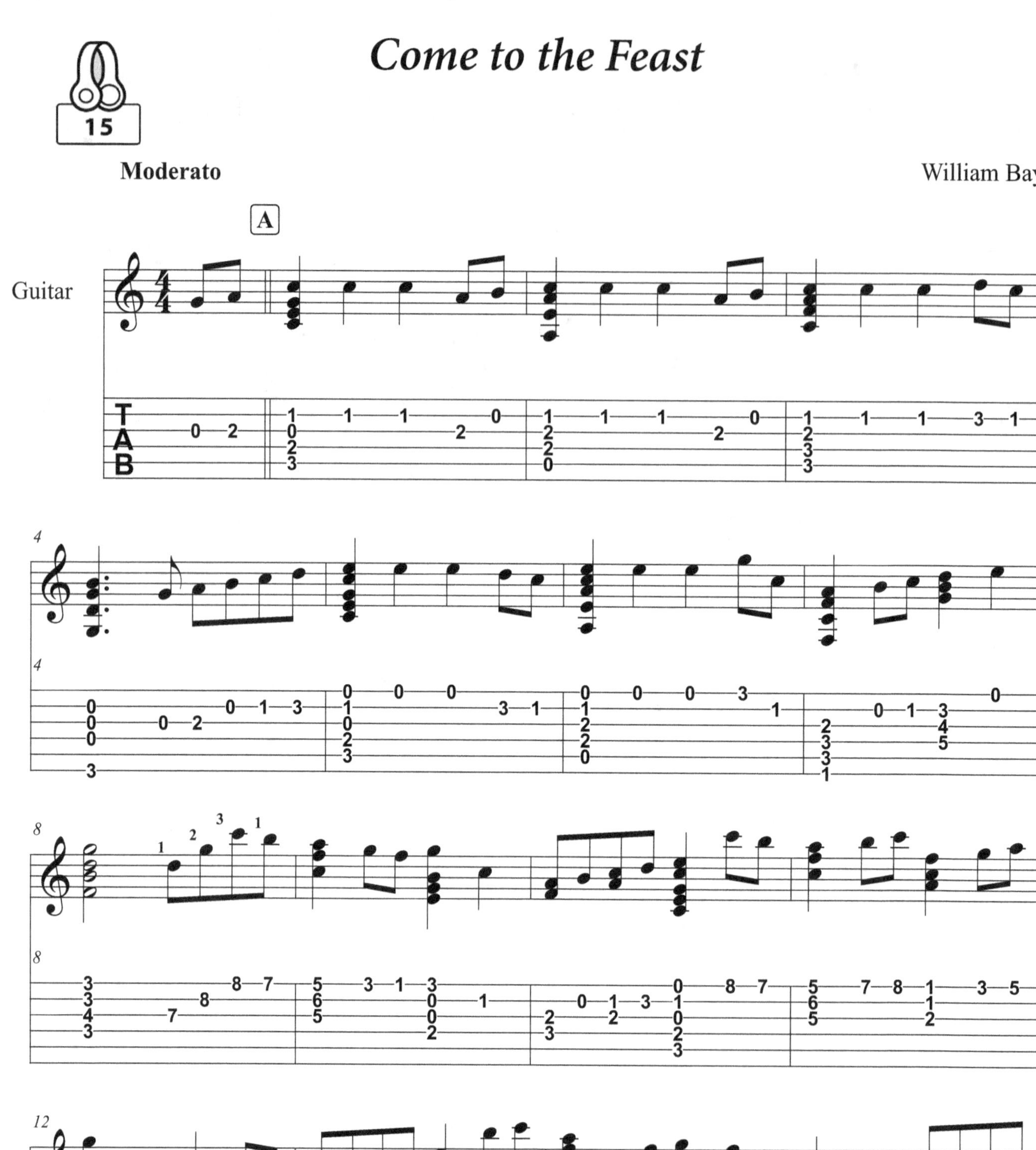

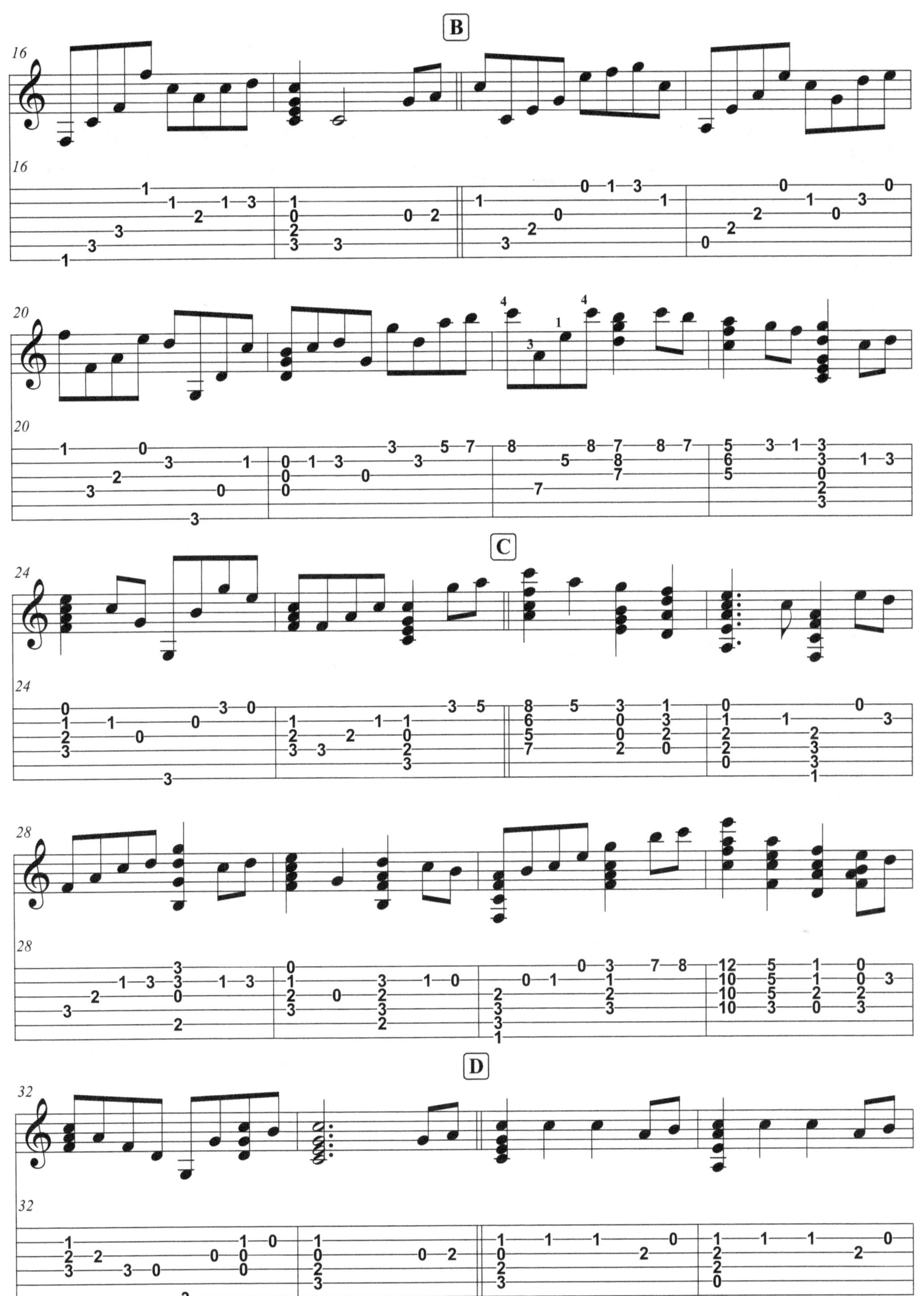

# *Adoro Devote*

*Dropped-D Tuning*

13th Century Plainsong

**Moderately Slow**

Guitar

# Bread of the World
## *Eucharistic Hymn*

*Dropped-D Tuning*

John S. B. Hodges, 1868

**Gently** ♩ = 80

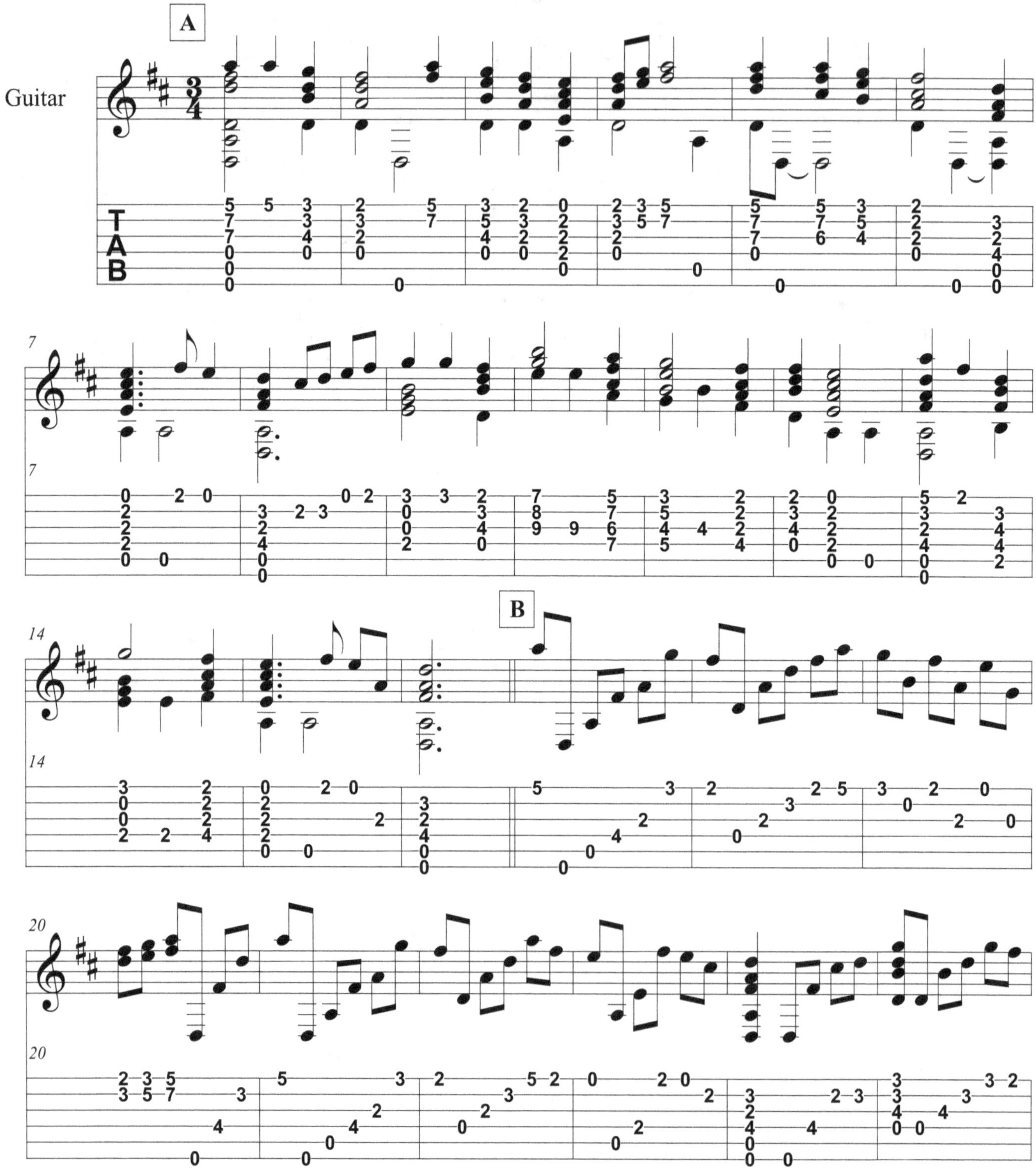

# Here, O My Lord, I See Thee Face to Face
## *Penitentia*

Edward Dearle, 1880

*Dropped-D Tuning*

**Slowly** ♩ = 84

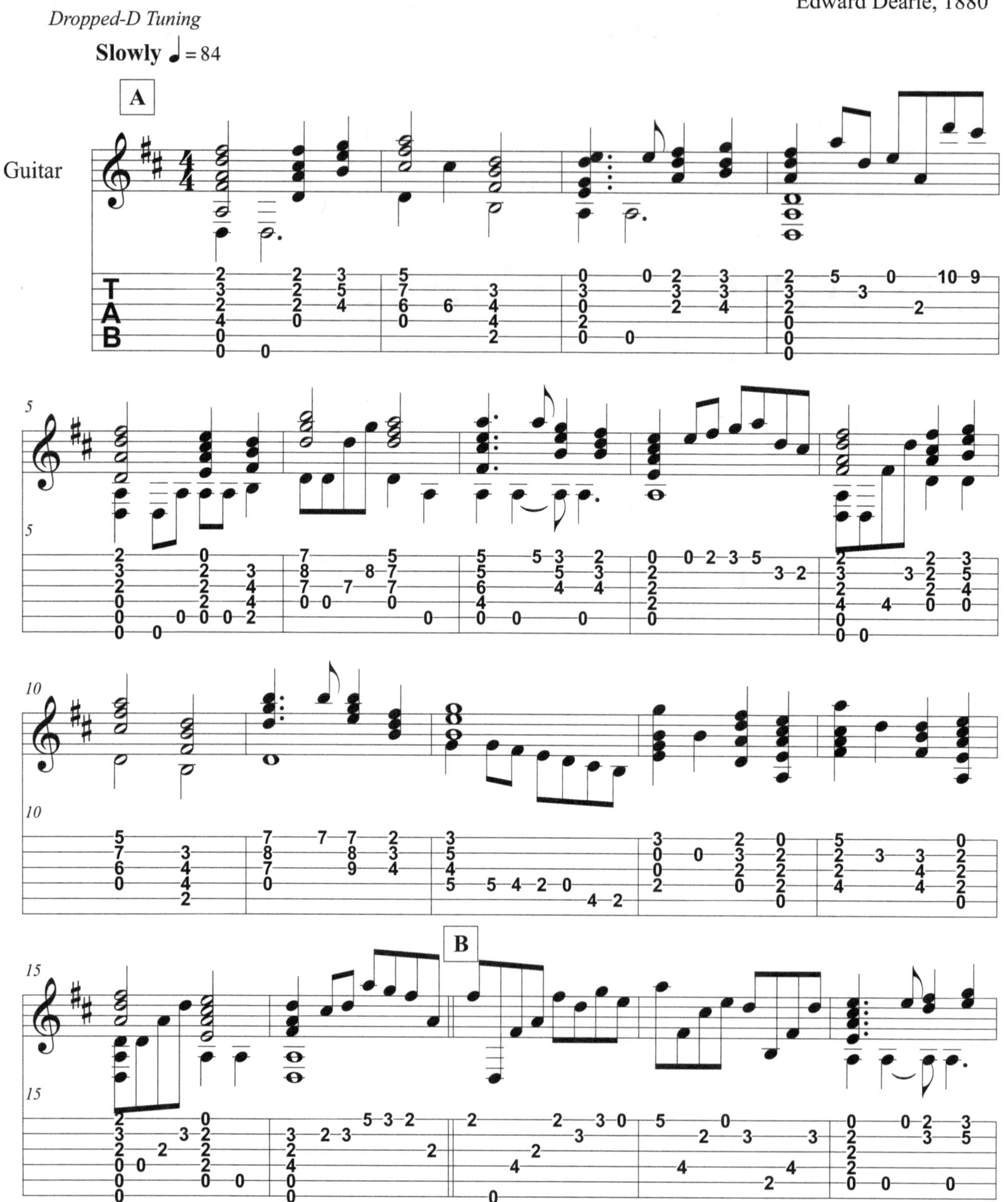

19
God Unseen Yet Ever Near
St. Flavian
Dropped-D Tuning
John Day's Psalter, 1562
Andante = 78
A
Guitar
T A B
B Boldly

# Turn Your Eyes Upon Jesus/He Is Lord

H. H. Lemmel

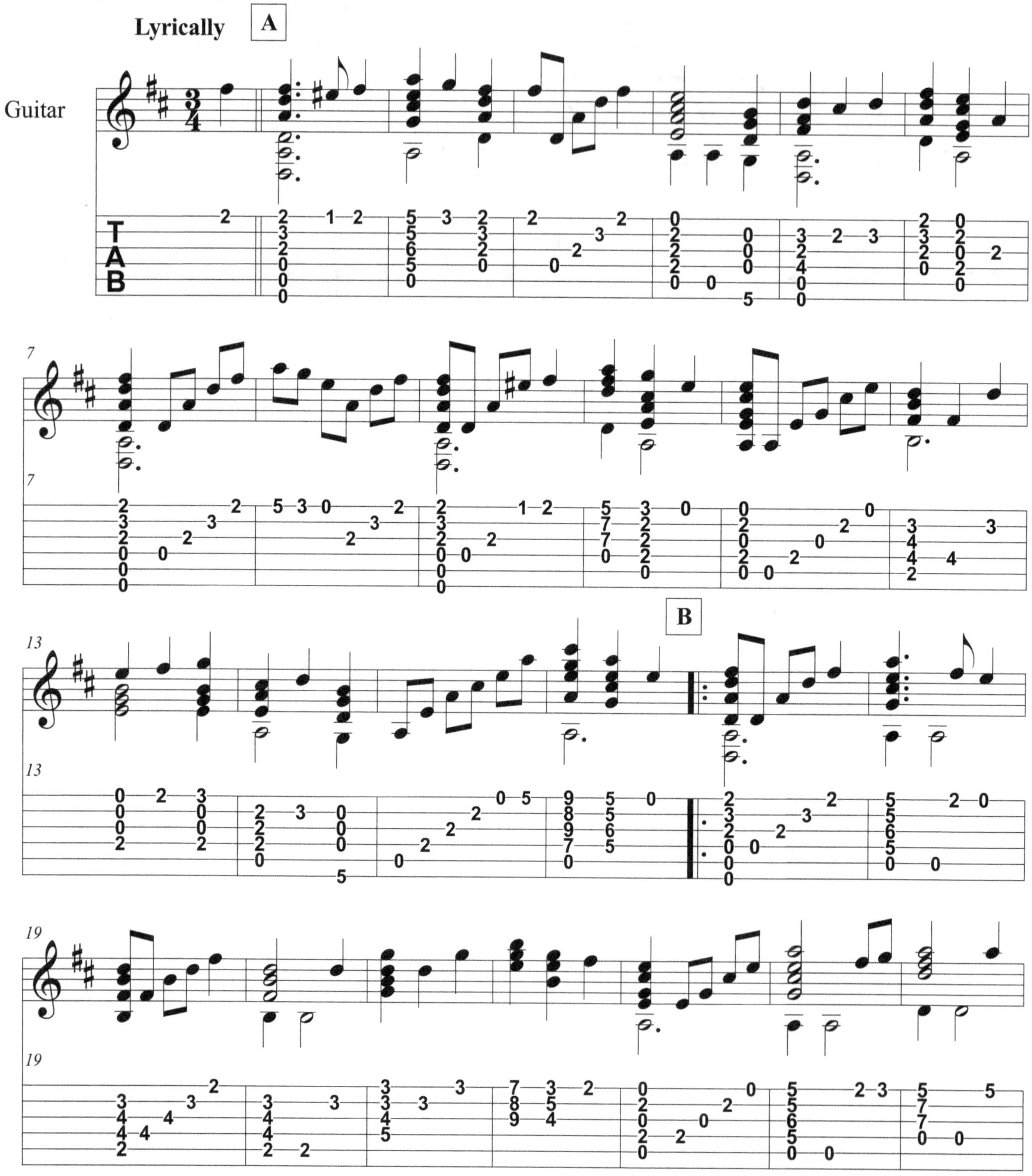

He is Lord

# What a Friend We Have in Jesus
## Converse

# Softly and Tenderly

*Dropped-D Tuning*

Will L. Thompson

**Freely**

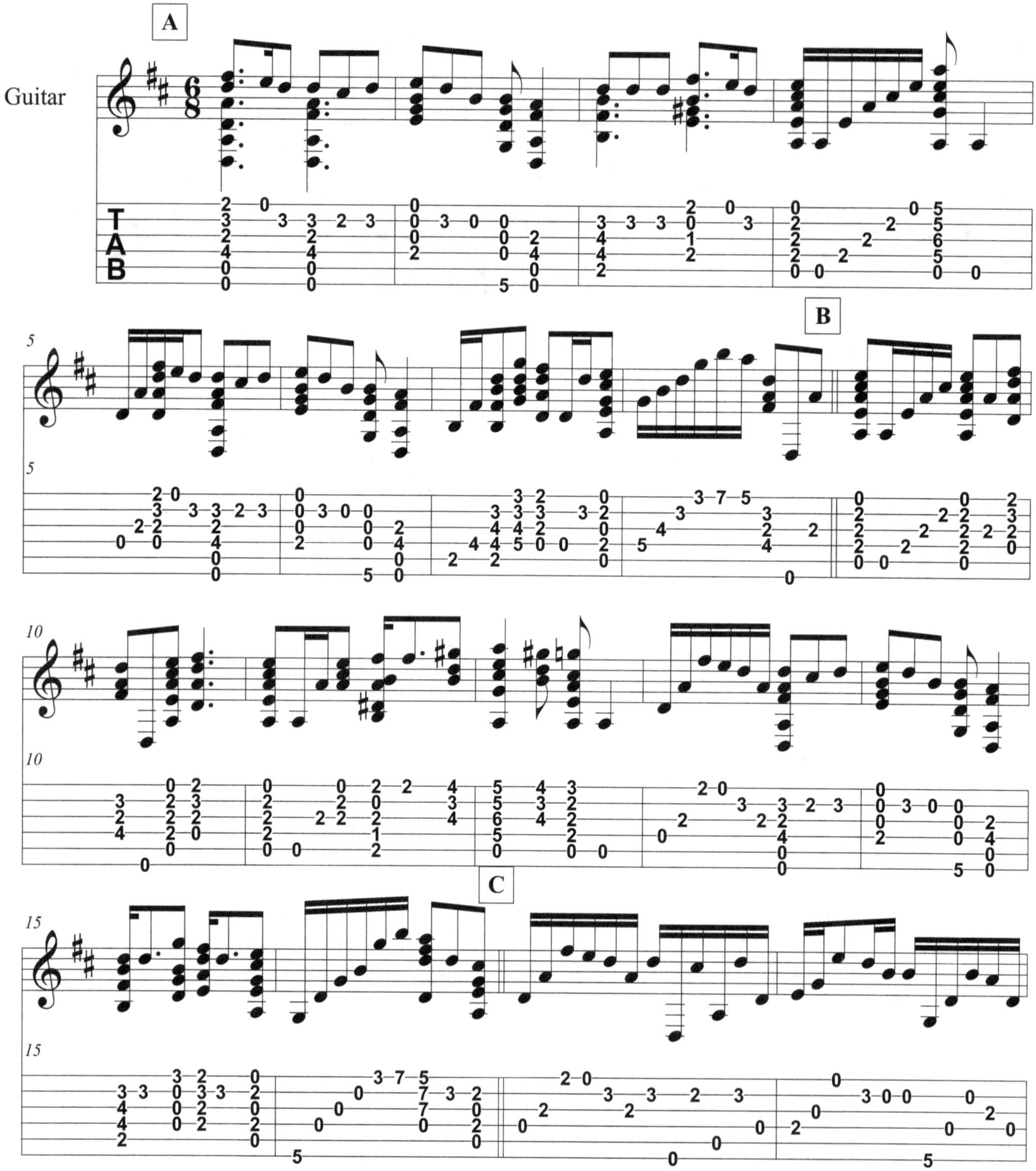

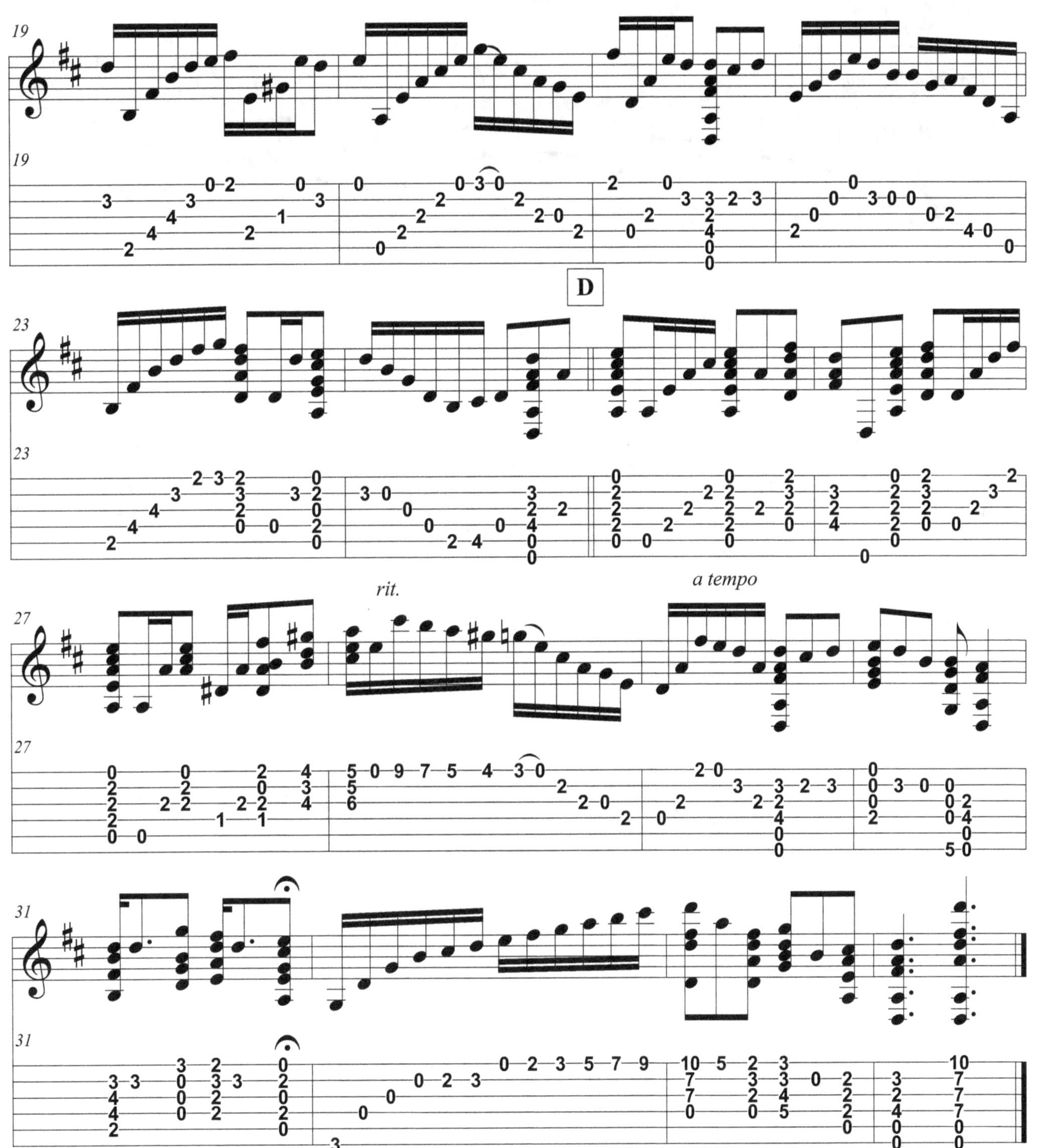
19
D
23
rit.
a tempo
27
31

# Let All Mortal Flesh Keep Silence
## *Picardy*

*Dropped-D Tuning*

French Hymn

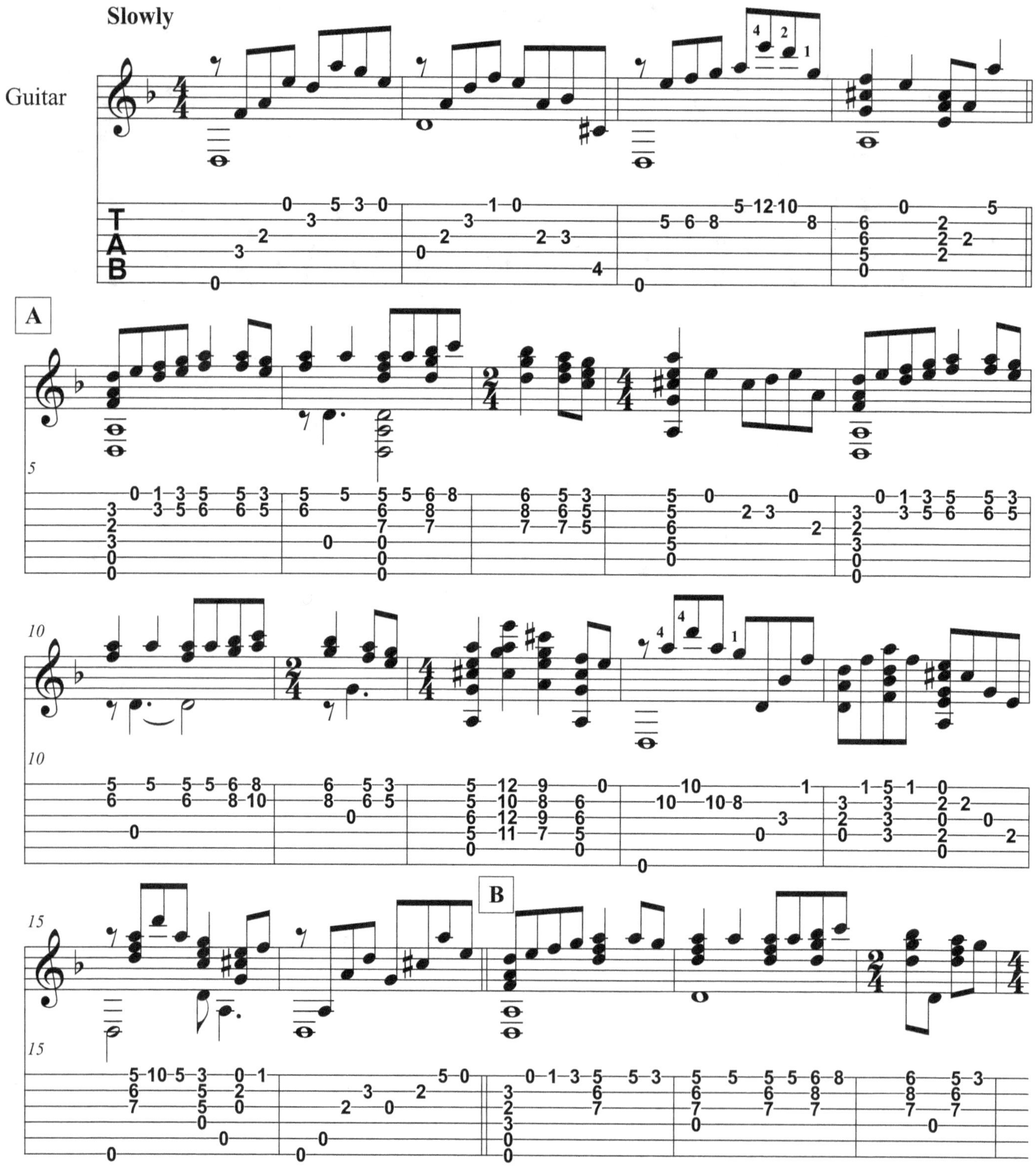

20
C
rubato
31

# We Give Thee Thanks

William Bay